THE GOSPEL
STORY

GREGORY DICKOW

The Gospel Story
©2003 by Gregory Dickow Ministries.
All rights reserved.

Unless otherwise noted, all Scripture quotations in this
volume are from the *King James Version* of the Bible.

Printed in the United States of America

For information, please write
Gregory Dickow Ministries,
P.O. Box 7000
Chicago, IL 60680

or visit us online at www.changinglives.org.

TABLE OF CONTENTS

THE GOSPEL STORY

Introduction

I have asked many people in the past, "Do you think you are going to Heaven?" and I have heard many people say, "Yes." When I ask them, "Why?" many say, "Because I am really not that bad of a person."

Just being "not that bad of a person" is not going to get someone into Heaven. You may not be as bad as Adolph Hitler, but you also may not be as good as Mother Theresa. So measuring ourselves by man's standards will always leave us falling short in one way or another.

We need to realize that we have all sinned. Romans 3:23 says, "All have sinned and fallen short of the glory of God." We have all come from Adam and Eve, and we are all born with a sinful nature. Our good works cannot get us into Heaven. The only way to get to Heaven is by putting our trust in the shed blood of Jesus.

I want you to understand this very simply and clearly so you can know you are going to Heaven. You need something to stand on, and that is the Word of God. I would like to make it very easy to understand by telling you the story of what God did for us. When you put your trust in what He did for you, you will not only go to Heaven whcn you die, but you will be changed forever, beginning today!

Let me tell you a story. It is a true story; in fact, it is *your* story.

THE HISTORY OF HUMANITY

Chapter One

It all began when God created man. He created Adam and Eve in His image and after His likeness, and He said to Adam and Eve, "I give you all of the Earth. This whole Earth belongs to you. You can rule over it. You can have dominion in it. But one thing you need to make sure you do—you need to honor Me by making sure not to eat from one tree in the Garden of Eden: the tree of the knowledge of good and evil. All these other trees you can eat from, but this one tree I do not want you to eat from. *I want you to trust Me.*"

Adam and Eve had the greatest life that any person could ever imagine and God said, "Just one thing I want you to do. Honor My Word and do not eat from the tree of the knowledge of good and evil."

Well, as we all know, they ate from that tree and they sinned against God. They gave in to Satan's temptation and they became connected to Satan and to a sinful nature. They listened to the devil rather than God. When they listened to him, he became their lord. Satan became their master, and God had to drive them out of the Garden of Eden. From that day forward, man lost his glory. From that day forward, man lost his relationship with God and his friendship with God. Man lost his authority over the earth and over the devil. Man became cursed from that day forward.

SIN INCREASED IN THE WORLD

Chapter Two

This is the history of what happened to Adam and Eve. Though it is all recorded in the book of Genesis, it is written plainly on your heart. In your heart of hearts, you know that it is true.

After Adam sinned, God said, "All right. Now that I have given my authority to Adam, and now he has given his authority over to the devil by obeying the devil, Satan is now the ruler of the world and he is in control of humanity." This is why the Bible calls the devil the god of this world's system. So all the men and women that were born to Adam and Eve took on a sinful nature, and sin kept increasing and increasing in the world. This is the story of humanity. This is what happened that fateful day.

Sin continued to increase and God said, "I am going to destroy the world." He destroyed the world with a flood, but He saved Noah, his wife and his children because Noah had faith in God. God told Noah how to build an ark and these eight people survived the flood. Then Noah's sons gave birth to their sons until Abraham was born and written about in the twelfth chapter of Genesis.

GOD MAKES A COVENANT WITH ABRAHAM

Chapter Three

At that point, God said to Abraham, "I am going to make a covenant with you, Abraham. A covenant is an agreement where you give me what you have and I will give you what I have." God told Abraham He was going to make him a father of nations and was going to bless him. He told him his descendants would take dominion of the earth back. But in exchange God said, "One thing I need from you, Abraham—your seed. I need the right to live on the earth. You are a man and you have the right to live on the earth. I am God. I do not have the right to live on the earth, because I gave authority to Adam, and Adam gave it to the devil."

You see God is a God of order and law. He couldn't just come back and invade the earth. So God said, "Abraham, I need your seed. I will tell you what I am going to do. If you will believe Me and if you will trust Me, I will give you a child when your wife is 90 years old. It will be a miracle. When your seed (child) grows, then I want you to offer that seed up to Me as a sacrifice."

You see a covenant is a contract that binds two parties to certain conditions, making the two into one (similar to a marriage). When God offered Abraham this covenant, he accepted it! And what happened? God gave Abraham riches, blessing, and authority, and Abraham gave God his seed—his son, Isaac.

Now God had a covenant with Abraham. He had an agreement with Abraham and He said, "Abraham, everything that you have belongs to Me now. And everything that I have belongs to you now. Whenever you need something you just ask Me, but I have one need now. I have the need to get back into the earth." So He said to Abraham, "Give Me your son." And Abraham obeyed. He offered up Isaac, but before Abraham sacrificed his son, God stopped him and said, "Now that I know I can trust you, because you have given Me your only son—your only begotten son—through his seed, I will now give birth to My Son in the earth, and His name shall be called Jesus. And He shall possess the gates of His enemies!" This is the story, and this is what happened.

GOD GIVES US HIS SON

Chapter Four

Abraham's seed, Isaac, had Jacob. Jacob had the twelve sons of Israel, and one of those sons was Judah. And Judah had sons and Judah's sons had sons and on and on it went, until a man named Joseph and a woman named Mary were born into the earth—both from the seed (or descendants) of Abraham. They became the parents of Jesus, but Jesus was conceived in Mary, the virgin, through the Holy Spirit. Jesus came to this earth and John the Baptist describes the gospel in one simple sentence: "Behold, the Lamb of God," he said, "who takes away the sin of the world" (John 1:29).

Do you realize Jesus could never have come into this earth had it not been for God making an agreement with Abraham? They made a blood covenant and Abraham gave God what he had. God gave Abraham what

He had, and now God (in the form of Jesus) had the right to come into this earth.

So the Holy Spirit conceived this child inside of the womb of Mary and He was born. 1 John 3:8 says He is the Son of God, and He came for this purpose: to take away sin and to destroy the works of the devil!

FORGIVENESS IN THE BLOOD OF JESUS

Chapter Five

Every human being that has ever been born on this earth has sin in their life. "We have all sinned," the Bible says, "and fallen short of the glory of God." Sin is doomed to hell and therefore **so are we** unless we receive forgiveness for our sins.

So Jesus came into the earth—not just to heal, not just to teach, and not just to feed the hungry—although he did all those things. He came into the earth to die on a cross. He stretched out His arms, died on a cross and His blood was spilled out. Why is it so important that His blood was shed? Because where there is no shedding of blood, there is no forgiveness of sins (Hebrews 9:22).

Blood represents a covenant: an exchange of life. When we were little kids, we would become blood brothers through pricking our fingers—through the shedding of blood. Well, when Jesus' blood was shed, He said, "I am going to be your blood brother now. If you will put your faith in Me," Jesus said, "I will be your blood brother and everything I have can be yours and everything you have can be Mine."

When blood was shed, the shed blood of Jesus washed away our sin. It washed away our guilt. It washed away all of our condemnation. It washed away our past before we ever had one! We all need His blood and we all need to be saved. You can't save yourself through your own works. You can't save yourself by being a good person. You can't save yourself by trying hard. You need a Savior and His name is Jesus. The Bible says in Romans 3:23, "ALL have sinned and fallen short of the glory of God." Romans 6:23 says, "The wages of sin is death, but the free gift of God is eternal life in Christ Jesus!"

BECOMING A
CHILD OF GOD

Chapter Six

Just as it only takes one murder to be a murderer, it only takes one sin to become a sinner. The good news about that is —in the same way—it only takes one act of righteousness for you to now become the righteousness of God. The Bible says in Romans 5:18 that **Jesus' one act of righteousness makes us**

all righteous, just like Adam's one act of sin made us all sinners.

You are not a "sinner" because you sinned; you are a "sinner" because you were a child of Adam. You are not "righteous" because you have done everything right. You are "righteous" because you now are a child of God. And the only way to become a child of God is not by singing a song, or by going to church, or by coming to the altar. **The only way to become a child of God is to be born again (John 1:12; John 3:3).**

The only way to become a child of your parents was to be born into this earth. And the only way to become a child of God is to be born again. When you are born again, God takes out your old sinful heart that you inherited from Adam and He gives you a new, holy heart that you inherit from Jesus—a new heart and a new beginning. You might ask, "If I have a new beginning then why do I still have problems?" We still have problems because God doesn't take out our mind. He doesn't give us a new mind. He takes out our heart and gives us a new heart, but we still have the same thinking that we had in the past. This is why He has given us His Word, the Bible—so we can change the way we think and renew our minds.

.

HOW TO BE BORN AGAIN

Chapter Seven

The Bible declares we were all children of the devil. But when we get born
again—when we accept Jesus Christ ac
our Lord and Savior—we become children
of God. John 1:12 says, "But as many as
received Him, to them He gave the right to
become children of God, even to those who
believe in His name." When we become chil-

dren of God, we have a new father—God becomes our Father. We have a new name. We have a new heart. We have a new beginning and we learn from the Bible how to walk with Him. 2 Corinthians 5:17 says, "If any man be in Christ, he is a new creature. The old things are passed away and all things have become new."

It is the blood of Jesus that washes us from sin and makes us whole all over again. Nothing but the blood can cleanse you. Nothing but the blood can change you. We are not talking about the blood of an animal. We are not talking about the blood of a lamb. We are not talking about the blood of a goat. We are talking about the blood of God Himself. For our sins and our sinfulness, God was willing to shed His very own blood!

Why do I serve God? Why do I follow Jesus? Do I do it because my parents told me to? No. Do I serve Him because it is easy all the time? No. I serve Him because if somebody would give their very life for me, that is one thing. But for God to give His very life for me, that is all together another thing! Romans 5:7 says, "For one will hardly die for a righteous man; though perhaps for a good man someone would dare even to die. But God demonstrates His own love toward us, in that while we were yet sinners, Christ died for us." It says, "would somebody die for a *good* man?" Hardly! But Jesus died for sinful men! He died for us while we were ungodly, while we were sinners, while we were full of darkness, while we were children of the devil, haters of God; lovers of pleasure rather than lovers of God.

While we were spitting in the face of Jesus through our attitude and through our actions, Jesus lovingly stretched out His arms for you and me, and was nailed to a cross for your forgiveness—for my forgiveness—so we could be a part of His family. I want you to think about this for a second. Think very clearly. Think very soberly. What do you put your trust in? When you die, do you know that there is only one reason God will let you into Heaven? And that one reason was because you turned from trusting anything else and put your trust in the shed blood of Jesus Christ. That cross is not a symbol of the past. That cross is the symbol of your future! It is on that cross—that tree, that heavy wood—where Jesus' blood flowed down. It is *that* blood that was shed that causes you and I to have access to go to Heaven.

If you have never made Jesus the Lord of your life, never surrendered your life completely to Him and said, "God take out my old heart and give me a new heart, and make me born again"—do it now. Or perhaps you have tried to be good and you thought, "If I am good enough, if I go to church, or if I do these things, then I will be saved." None of that will save you. Only the blood of Jesus will save you. If you are not absolutely sure of your salvation, I want to lead you in this prayer of faith and something miraculous is going to happen in your heart. Pray this out loud:

"Heavenly Father, I invite Jesus Christ into my life as my Lord and as my Savior. I believe Jesus died for my sins. His blood was shed so that I could be forgiven and I believe that He has been raised from the dead. I declare Jesus Christ is my Lord from this moment forward. I receive the forgiveness of my sins through the blood of Jesus. Take out my old heart, Lord, and give me a new heart, a new spirit, a new life and I will follow You, with Your help, by Your grace, all the days of my life. In Jesus' Name."

Now listen, that is just the beginning! There is something that God wants to happen in your life. He wants you to grow. He wants you to move forward. He doesn't want you to live like you used to live. When we get born again we have a new life. But with that new life, we need a new lifestyle. If you have just made Jesus your Lord, contact my Prayer Center at 847-645-9700 and let me know. I want to help you.

Next Steps:

Now thank Him for making you His child. And don't doubt! You are a child of God right now! I John 3:2 says, "Beloved *now* are we the children of God."

Read the Bible and talk to God. God has a great plan for your life. He loves you and wants the best for you. You are His child now. You are in the family of God today. Your life will never be the same again!

It is my pleasure to welcome you into the family of God!

I made Jesus the Lord of my life today!

Signature _____

Date _____

About the Author

Gregory Dickow is the host of *"The Power to Change Today,"* a dynamic television show seen throughout the world, reaching a potential half a billion households. He is also the founder and Senior Pastor of *Life Changers International Church*, a diverse and thriving congregation in the Chicago area with several thousand in weekly attendance.

Known for his ability to communicate the power and principles of God's Word clearly and concisely, Gregory Dickow lives to see the lives of people dramatically changed forever.

Pastor Dickow is also the host of *"Ask the Pastor"* a live radio show reaching the world through radio and the internet with live callers asking hard-hitting questions about their real-life problems. Gregory Dickow is reaching people personally, encouraging them and empowering them to succeed in every area of life.

Other Books Available by Pastor Gregory Dickow

- Acquiring Beauty
- Breaking the Power of Inferiority
- Conquering Your Flesh
- Financial Freedom
- How to Hear the Voice of God
- How to Never Be Hurt Again
- Taking Charge of Your Emotions
- The Power to Change Anything
- Winning the Battle of the Mind

Audio Series available by Pastor Gregory Dickow

- Financial Freedom: Strategies for a Blessed Life
- How to Pray & Get Results
- Love Thyself
- Mastering Your Emotions
- Winning The Battle Of Your Mind
- Don't Be Afraid Of The Dark
- Supernatural Success: You Cannot Fail

You can order these and many other life-changing materials by calling toll-free 1-888-438-5433.

For more information about Gregory Dickow Ministries and a free product catalog, please visit *www.changinglives.org*

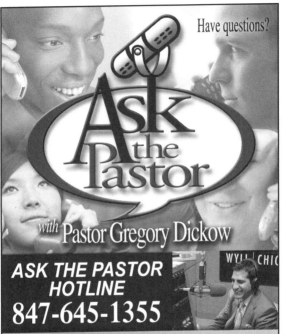

Have questions?

Ask the Pastor

with Pastor Gregory Dickow

ASK THE PASTOR HOTLINE
847-645-1355

Ask the Pastor with Gregory Dickow airs LIVE every weekday from 5:00pm to 7:00pm Central Time on AM-1160 WYLL in Chicago and is streamed live via the internet. You can hear the show by visiting gregorydickow.org and clicking on the "Listen Live" link. If you need Bible-based answers to your real-life questions, *call Ask the Pastor today!*

VISIT US ONLINE AT

gregorydickow.org

FOR MORE LIFE-CHANGING RESOURCES!

OTHER LIFE-CHANGING BOOKS

Taking Charge of Your Emotions: In this life chang-
ing book, you will discover: how to change the way you feel, how to get off
the emotional rollercoaster, the root of depression and all negative emotions,
freedom from anger, stress, and much more!

Conquering Your Flesh: No longer do you have to put up with
your flesh controlling your life and suffering the consequences of it. Begin
experiencing the freedom you've always wanted by conquering your flesh!

Breaking the Power of Inferiority: In this book you will
learn the signs of inferiority, how to break the cycle of insecurity, the difference
between dominion & domination, the solution to jealousy, how to reign in life
as a king and much more!

How to Never Be Hurt Again: Learn the wrong response
to hurt, the right response to hurt, the simple steps to being free, how to over-
come past hurts in your life, and how to release supernatural favor in your life.

Winning the Battle of Your Mind: The devil has been
defeated! So why do we still struggle sometimes? The answer is right between
our ears! It is our thinking that paves the way for victory or defeat in our lives.

Financial Freedom: Walk in your God-given right to financial
freedom and debt-free living! Discover the 10 simple steps to getting out and
staying out of debt and experience the perfect will of God in your finances!

How to Hear the Voice of God Today!: By recog-
nizing the voice of God, you will discover the peace, security and confidence
that come from your loving Father! Don't live another moment without knowing
how to hear the voice of God—today!